Günter Gerngross • Herbert Puchta

PLAYWAY 3 TO ENGLISH

Activity Book

Arbeitsmaterialien für den Englischunterricht
Altersgruppe: 3. Schuljahr
Illustrationen: Svjetlan Junaković

W0401203

Helbling

Klett

Unit 1 Back to school

1 Listen and point.

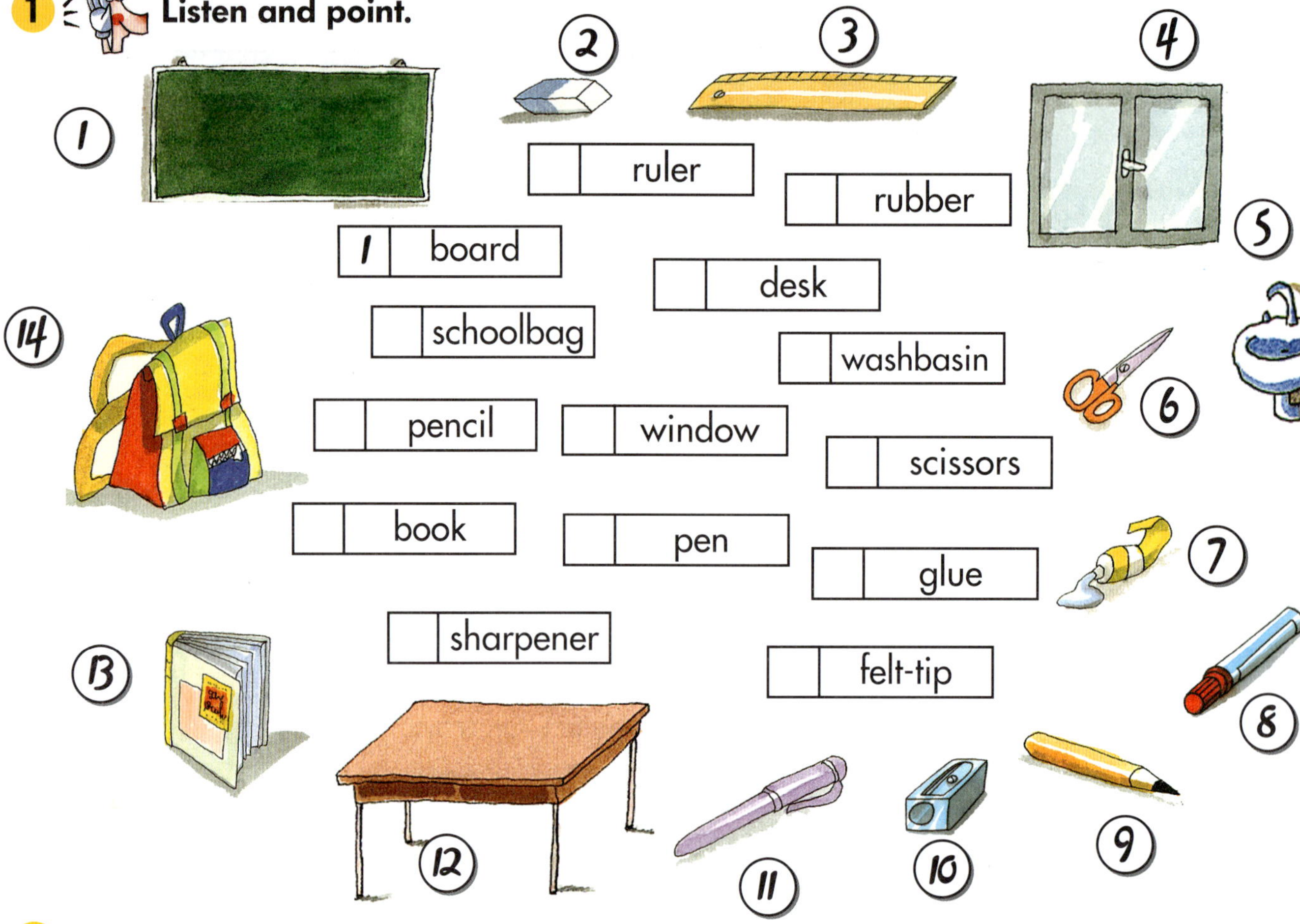

2 Match the pictures and the words.

3 Listen and draw lines.

4 **Count and speak.**

5 **Say the sentences.**

Put on	Have	Get	Get out	Wash	Put on

of bed. your face. some toast with jam.

your jeans. your T-shirt. your schoolbag.

Back to school

6 Watch the video. Listen. Then stick in the missing pictures. p. 45

The new girl

Shoot, Sonia!

Brilliant! Cool!

OK, children. Let's go back to the classroom. The score is 4 – 0.

Have an apple, Sonia.
Oh, that's nice. Thanks.

Pets

1 Find the pets. Then tick true or false.

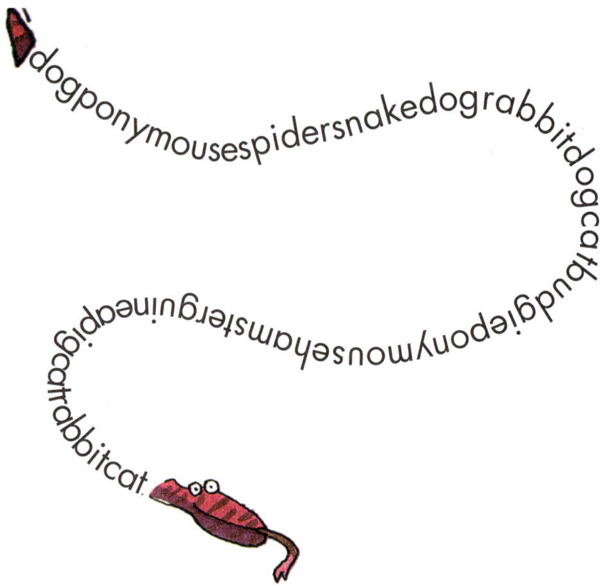

	True	False
There are three dogs.		
There are two hamsters.		
There is one mouse.		
There are four guinea pigs.		
There is one spider.		
There are three ponies.		
There are two rabbits.		
There is one budgie.		
There are two cats.		
There is one snake.		

2  **Listen and stick in the animals. Find the hidden word.**

p. 47

	blue	green	red	yellow	pink
1					
2					
3					

3 Read and colour.

The budgies are blue and green.

The guinea pig is orange, white and brown.

The rabbit is pink and grey.

The pony is black and white.

The snake is red and yellow.

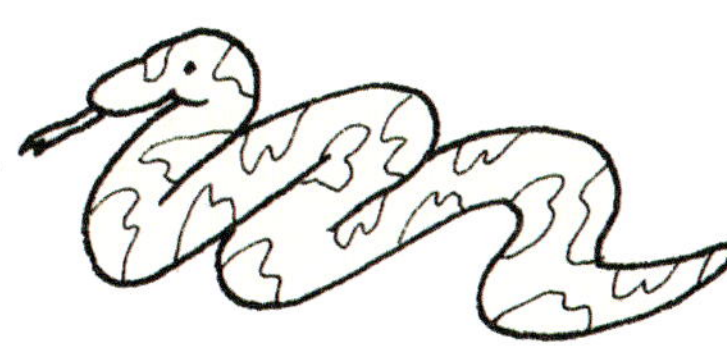

4  **Listen and join the dots.**

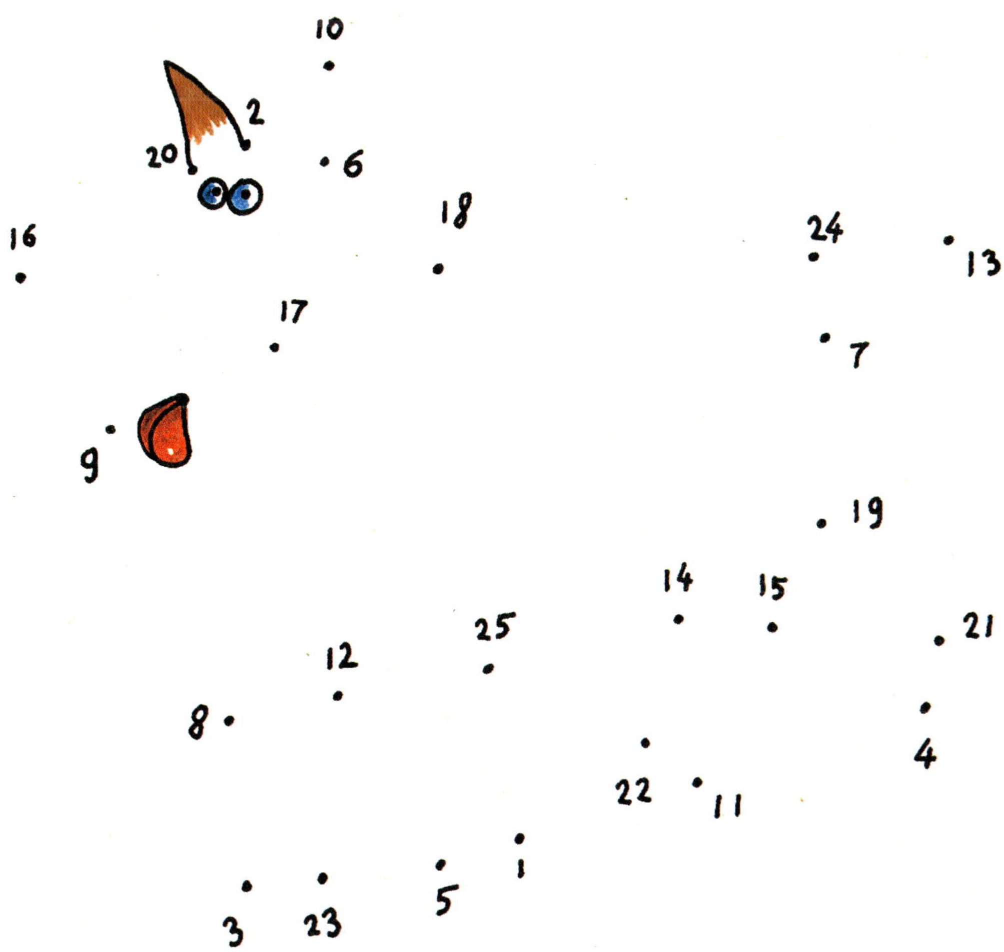

Pets

5 Follow the lines and answer the questions. Fill in ☺ or ☹.

Yes, she has. ☺	**No, she hasn't.** ☹
Yes, he has.	**No, he hasn't.**

Has Emma got a dog?	☺	Has Lisa got a pony?	
Has Alex got a snake?	☹	Has Paul got a cat?	
Has Joe got a mouse?		Has Ben got two rabbits?	
Has Eve got two guinea pigs?		Has Diana got a hamster?	

I'm scared

1 Tick the correct sentences.

☐ He isn't scared of snakes.

☐ He is scared of snakes.

☐ He isn't scared of spiders.

☐ He is scared of spiders.

☐ She isn't scared of frogs.

☐ She is scared of frogs.

☐ He isn't scared of dogs.

☐ He is scared of dogs.

☐ They aren't scared of mice.

☐ They are scared of mice.

☐ They aren't scared of ghosts.

☐ They are scared of ghosts.

2  **Listen and fill in for scared and for not scared.**

Sheila						
Alan						
Nicola						
Bill						

I'm scared

3 Watch the video. Listen. Then stick in the missing pictures. p. 47

Max is scared

But the dog is not happy about that.
Max climbs a tree.
What a stupid dog.
Come down, Max.
I can't, I'm so scared.
Jump, Max.
Here I come!

I'm scared

4 **What are you scared of? Tick the correct answers.**

	Yes, I am.	No, I'm not.
Are you scared of mice?		
Are you scared of ghosts?		
Are you scared of monsters?		
Are you scared of dogs?		
Are you scared of spiders?		
Are you scared of snakes?		
Are you scared of witches?		
Are you scared of skeletons?		

5 **Read the text. Draw the missing things.**

I'm not scared of ☐ (mice).

I'm not scared of ☐ (dogs).

I'm not scared of ☐ (snakes)

and I'm not scared of ☐ (spiders),

but I'm scared of the monster under my bed.

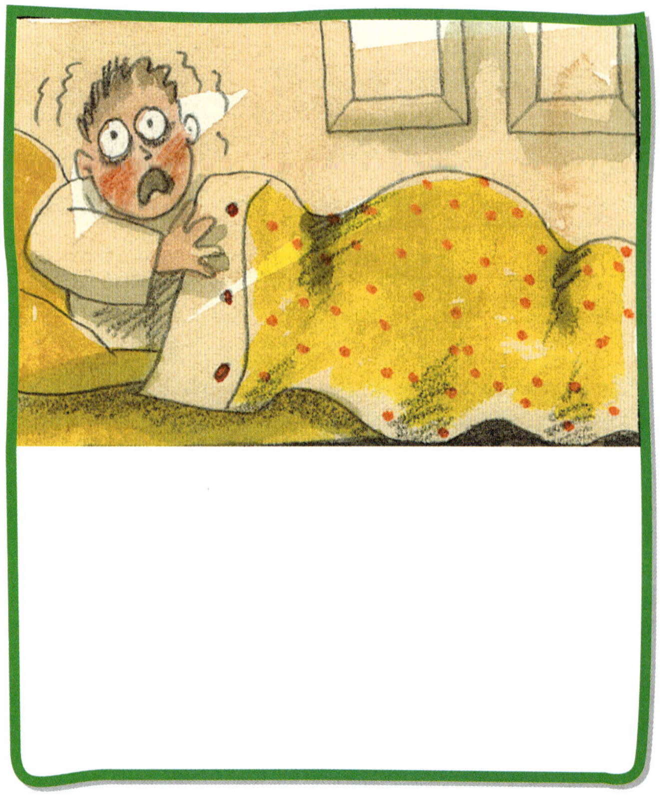

6 **Tick the correct answers.**  **Then listen and check.**

Max and the dog

Max is in his neighbour's
☐ garden.
☐ house.

He ☐ is / ☐ sees a dog.

The dog ☐ runs to / ☐ looks at Max.

Max is ☐ happy. / ☐ scared.

He ☐ runs away. / ☐ goes away.

He ☐ climbs / ☐ sees a tree.

Max ☐ is / ☐ isn't very scared.

The dog ☐ goes away. / ☐ is scared.

Max climbs ☐ down the tree. / ☐ down the desk.

What's the time?

1 Listen and draw.

2 Watch the video. Listen. Then stick in the missing texts. p. 49

Midnight on the farm

Unit 4

What's the time?

It's one o'clock.
?
Stop!
The farmer is coming.
What's this?
Playing cards?
?

What's the time?

3 Listen. Can you find out what the time is?

1	2	3	4	5	6	7	8	9	10	11	12	13	14	15

My body

1 Find the words.

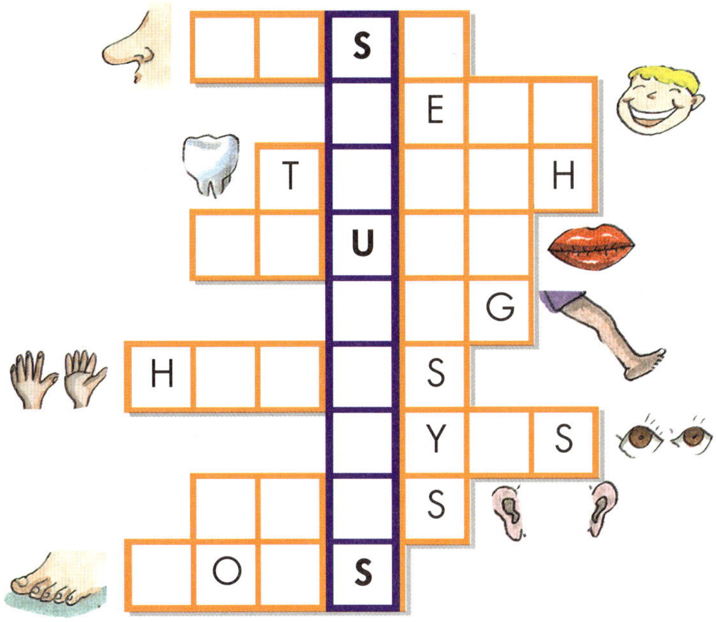

2  **Listen. Complete the text. Then colour the monkey.**

blue left hair mouth right eyes pink feet left orange arm ear green

His ______ is yellow. His ______ ear is green, and his right ______ is red. His ______ are blue and his nose is ______. His ______ is red.

His ______ arm is ______ and his right ______ is pink. His hands are ______. His ______ leg is grey, and his left leg is ______. His ______ are yellow.

My body

3 Watch the video. Listen. Then stick in the missing pictures. p. 49

Mr Crocodile and Dr Kangaroo

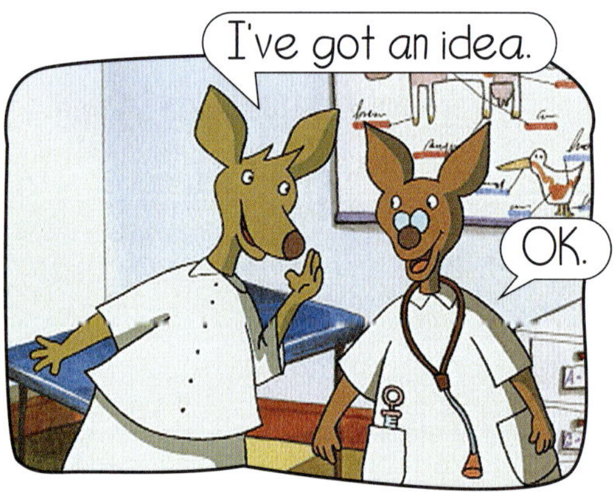

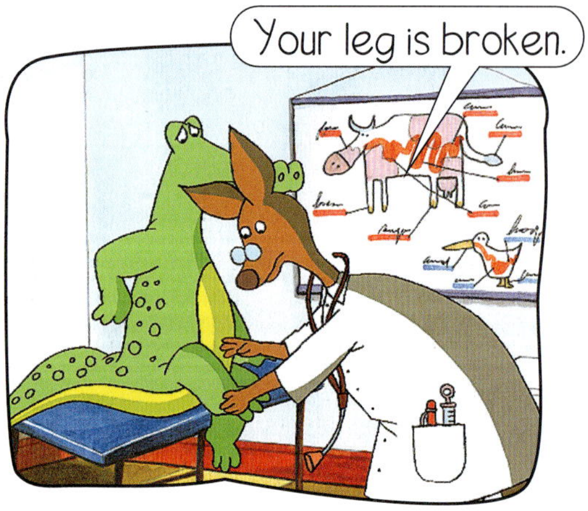

What a lovely kangaroo.
Now the crocodile is very hungry.
Catch me! Catch me! Crocodile, catch me!
Ouch!
Sleep well, Mr Crocodile.
The leg's OK.
I've finished.
?
?
?
?
Your leg's OK. You can go home now.
Thank you.
Thank you, Doctor. Thank you.

My body

4 **Draw a picture of the thief in Max's garden.**

5 **Stick in the missing words.** p. 51

This man has stolen my flowers:

He has got a [?] mouth,
[?] [?] hair and
big [?]. His nose is [?]
and his [?] are blue.

Help me find the man!

Free time

1 **Listen and stick in the pictures. Then stick in the words.** p. 51

On Monday he

On Tuesday he

On Wednesday he

On Thursday he

On Friday he

On Saturday he

And on Sunday he rests.

2 Watch the video. Listen. Then stick in the missing texts. p. 51

Max on holiday

Aaaaah!
?
Brrrr. It's cold.
?
Aargggh!
?
But not Max ...
?

Free time

3 Play the game with a friend. You need two dice. Throw the dice and complete the words.

2 = A	7 = R
3 = E	8 = S
4 = F	9 = U
5 = H	10 = D
6 = I	11 = Y
12 = Miss a turn.	

MONDAY	M	O	N						
TUESDAY	T								
WEDNESDAY	W			N					
THURSDAY	T								
FRIDAY									
SATURDAY			T						
SUNDAY			N						

Clothes

1 Look at the children's clothes. Read and write the names.

Alicia

Evan

Ann

Larry

Elisa

Will

His cap is blue. His shirt is orange. His pullover is green. His jeans are blue and his shoes are grey. His belt is black. His schoolbag is yellow and green.

What's his name?

____

Her sweatshirt is red. Her jeans are blue. Her trainers are white and green. Her schoolbag is blue and red.

What's her name?

____

His cap is blue. His shirt is white and blue. His jeans and his boots are grey. His belt is black. His schoolbag is green.

What's his name?

____

Her anorak is yellow. Her jeans are blue. Her trainers are orange, grey and blue. Her schoolbag is yellow.

What's her name?

____

His cap is green. His shirt is orange and blue. His jeans are blue and his shoes are grey. His schoolbag is red.

What's his name?

____

Her sweatshirt is red. Her jeans are blue. Her trainers are white and grey. Her schoolbag is blue.

What's her name?

____

Unit 7

Clothes

2 **Watch the video. Listen. Then stick in the missing pictures.** p. 53

The hats in the attic

It doesn't fit Prince Gregory.

?

?

Hurrah, it fits you!
Prince Benny, marry me.

Marry you? I can't.
I'm only 10.
Linda, help me!

Take the hat off!

?

Benny, Linda! What are you doing in the attic?
And what's that?
Ha ha ha!

Clothes

3 Colour and speak.

Birthdays

1 Circle the names of the months. Write.

1 *January*..................

2 ....

3 ....

4 ....

5 ....

6 ....

7 ....

8 ....

9 ....

10 ....

11 ....

12 ....

2 Find the twelve months.

A	U	G	U	S	T	L	M	N	F
L	P	L	F	Q	P	U	A	O	S
D	E	C	E	M	B	E	R	V	E
U	T	N	B	S	S	M	C	E	P
S	C	A	R	E	D	A	H	M	T
J	A	N	U	A	R	Y	J	B	E
A	F	S	A	D	M	X	U	E	M
T	A	P	R	I	L	H	N	R	B
J	U	L	Y	T	I	R	E	D	E
N	R	X	O	C	T	O	B	E	R

Birthdays

3 **Find out the children's names. When are their birthdays?**

☆ = a
● = b
✧ = h
❒ = d
■ = e
○ = c
✱ = l
✤ = i
◗ = u
✺ = y
✦ = m
▼ = r
▲ = s

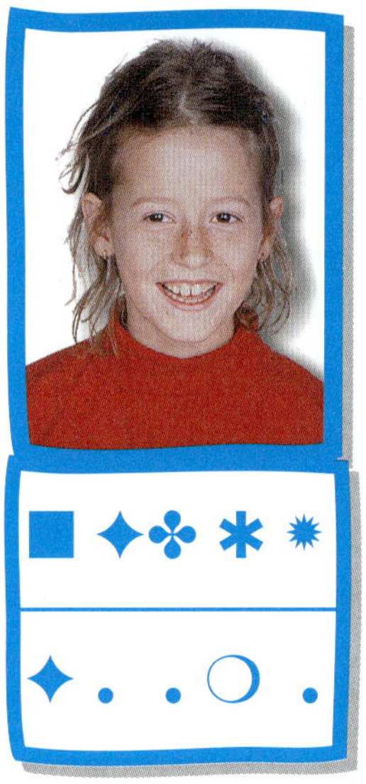

4 **Guess and speak.**

1. This month begins with 'A'. It has five letters.
2. This month has twenty-eight or twenty-nine days.
3. This month has eight letters. It begins with 'N'.
4. This month begins with 'A'. It has six letters.
5. This month has nine letters.
6. This month has five letters. It begins with 'M'.
7. This month has three letters.
8. This month begins with 'D'.

3 **Look at the puzzle pieces on page 55. Guess where the following things are: the schoolbag, the ball, the sweater, the umbrella, the TV, the books, the cat, the socks.**

4 **Now cut out the puzzle pieces. Stick them in 3. Complete the sentences.** p. 55

The schoolbag	
The ball	
The sweater	
The socks	
The umbrella	
The books	
The TV	
The cat	

At home

5 Spot the differences. Fill in the missing words. Then listen and check.

wardrobe on are next to grey chair are chair

The curtains in picture A ___________ green. In picture B they are blue.
In picture A the ___________ is in front of the desk. In picture B it is
in front of the ___________. The wardrobe in picture A is brown.
In picture B it is ___________. In picture A the jeans are on the bed.
In picture B they ___________ on the chair. In picture A the pen is
under the ___________. In picture B it is ___________ the desk.
In picture A the lamp is on the desk. In picture B it is ______________ the desk.

What do you collect?

1 Look at the picture and answer the questions. Then tick the right answer.

	Yes, he does.	No, he doesn't.
Does Simon collect bells?	✔	
Does he collect shells?		✔
Does he collect caps?		
Does he collect flags?		
Does he collect CDs?		
Does he collect watches?		
Does he collect books?		
Does he collect guitars?		

2 Look at the picture. Write the sentences.

Alice *collects sunglasses.*

She *doesn't collect books.*

She ______________________.

She ______________________.

She ______________________.

She ______________________.

What do you collect?

3 Watch the video. Listen. Then stick in the missing texts. p. 55

The circus

?
Sorry, I can't. I'm playing basketball this afternoon.
Linda, I've got an idea.
?
The next day, they put up a poster in class.
Oh, no! Look at the lion!
Oh, he's hungry.
And the monkey. He looks so sad.
The next day, lots of children help Linda and Benny.
?
Thank you! Thank you all!

What do you collect?

4 Listen and colour the numbers. Find out what Hector does not collect.

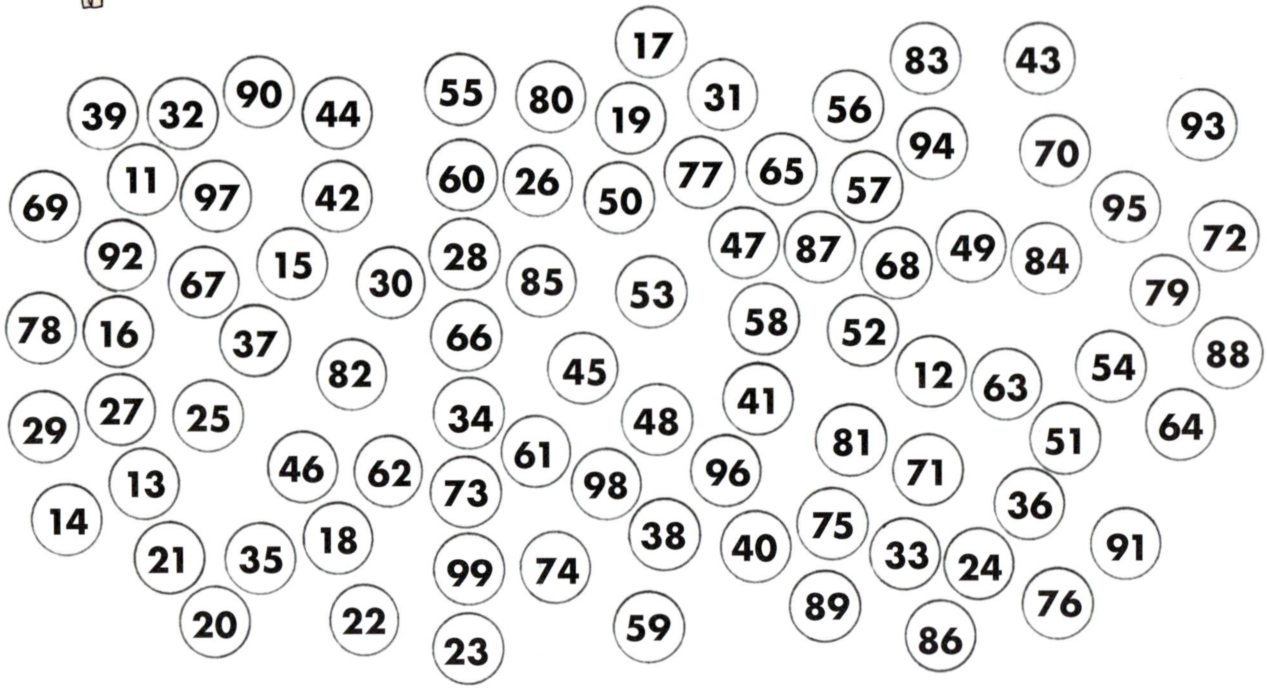

5 Play the game.

Food and drink

1 Listen and draw: ☺ or ☹

2 Play a guessing game.

3 Watch the video. Listen. Then stick in the missing texts. p. 55

Orange juice for Max

Hi, Linda.
Hi, Sally.
?
Careful, Benny.
There's a bee on your head.
Close your eyes.
Don't move.
?
?
I'll get you!

Food and drink

4  **Listen and fill in the letters.**

Mum = M
Benny = B
Max = X
Dad = D
Linda = L

Main course		Vegetables		Drinks	

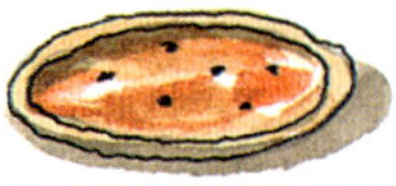					

		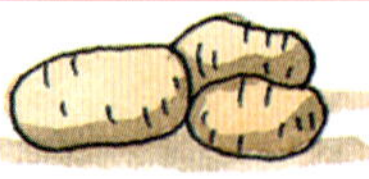			
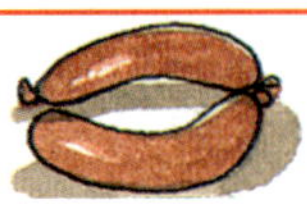					

5 **How many true sentences can you make? How many lies can you make?**

Unit 1 Back to school

6 p. 4

Unit 2 Pets

2 p. 6

Unit 3 I'm scared

3 p. 10

Unit 4 What's the time?

2 p. 15

Head and shoulders, knees and toes ...	Here it is.	Where are the cards? Am I dreaming?
It's quarter past twelve.	Great! Brilliant! You're the winner.	Where's the football?
It's quarter to one.	It's your turn, Duck.	What's that!?

Unit 5 My body

3 p. 20

Unit 5 My body

5 p. 22

black	wide	ears
short	eyes	small

Unit 6 Free time

1 p. 23

plays volleyball.
plays football.
swims in the river.
plays tennis.
rides his horse.
rides his bike.

2 p. 24

On Sunday, they go skiing.	On Friday, Max goes ice-skating.
On Saturday, Linda, Benny and Max have a snowball fight.	On Thursday, he goes snowboarding.
On Wednesday, Max goes sledging.	On Monday, Max makes a snowman.
On Tuesday, he goes curling.	

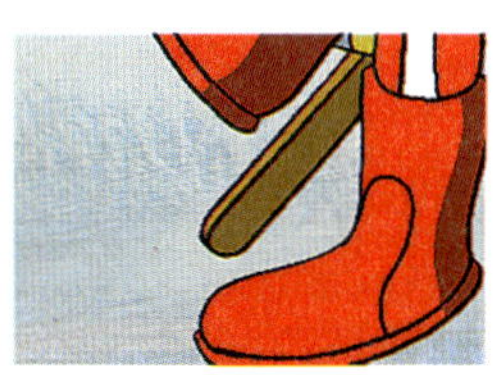
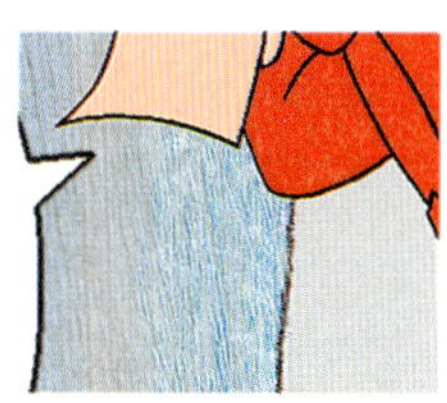

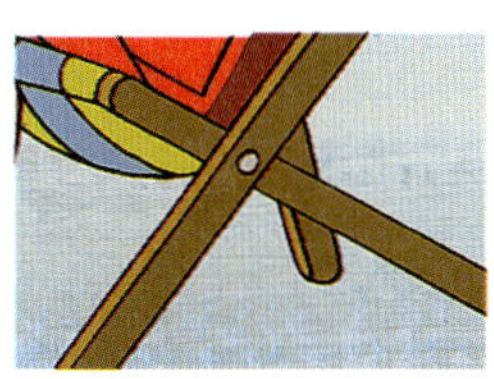
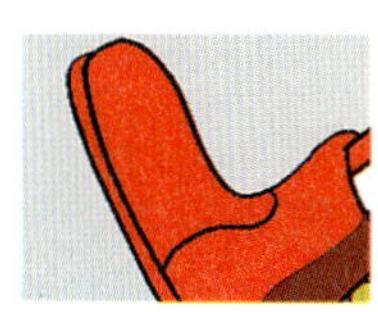

Unit 9 At home

3 p. 35

4 p. 35

is on the sofa.	is in front of the wardrobe.
is in front of the wardrobe.	is in the washbasin.
are on the lamp.	is next to the cupboard.
are under the table.	is under the bed.

Unit 10 What do you collect?

3 p. 38

Now there is enough food for the animals.	Because we haven't got enough money for food.
There's a woman over there.	Sorry, I've got no time.
Can you help us?	They take lots of photos.
Linda and Benny have an idea.	At the weekend, Linda and Benny go to see the animals.

Unit 11 Food and drink

3 p. 42

What a lovely dog.	Thank you.	Can I have a lemonade?
Thank you, Max.	OK, Max.	Here you are.
You can open your eyes. The bee's gone.	No, Max. Two is enough.	